D0912015

A Truce With Fantasy

A Truce With Fantasy

Poems by

Bill Mayer

Kelsay Books

© 2015 Bill Mayer. All rights reserved. This material may not be reproduced in any form, published, reprinted, recorded, performed, broadcast, rewritten or redistributed without the explicit permission of Bill Mayer. All such actions are strictly prohibited by law.

Cover Art: Bill Mayer

ISBN 13:978-0692445594

Kelsay Books
Aldrich Press
www.kelsaybooks.com

For Jane

Acknowledgements

Already After 4 was published in *Visions International*
Back and Forth was published in *Danse Macabre*
Time and Beauty was published in Omniverse, *Omnidawn Online*
After Horace was published by *Visions International*
Poem Beginning and Ending with Lines from James Agee was
    published by *Visions International*
In the Seventeenth Century was published by Danse Macabre
Silence is Imaginary Because the World Never Stops Making
Noise was published by *Visions International.*

Cover Art: Photograph of the Eureka Valley, California
    by Bill Mayer
Inside cover, by John R. Neill, illustration from Ozma of Oz,
    by L. Frank Baum, 1906
Photograph of the author by Jane McKinne-Mayer

Also by Bill Mayer:
The Uncertainty Principle
Longing
The Deleted Family
Articulate Matter

DOROTHY AFLOAT IN THE HEN-COOP

Contents

Part 3   The Time Between Worlds

Part 4   Learning To Breathe Again

Part 5   Breakfast In Bed

Part 6

Part 7   A Truce With Fantasy

Part 1
A World Without I

Poem beginning and ending with lines from James Agee

High summer holds the earth, the fog drips
quietly in the night. The trains, their horns
a distant orchestra, speak only of the past,
and are comforting. Time is still,
with the birch seeds falling, no,
not falling, at ease in their slow drift down,
around us, in our hair, on the floors
and pillows, like at my great grandmother's
home, the yellowed curtains, the light
filtering in as though through dust,
old Los Angeles in the quiet September heat.
I am lost in the past, at the ranch
out in Woodland Hills, long gone,
among the rusting machinery
and high, dried grasses in the back,
the creatures, spiders, squirrels, snakes,
cats, dogs, a horse that lived there,
the fields, and trees I could climb,
resting in a crotch of branches, the leaves
hiding me, reading, drifting, the entire
visible world flowing as water, as air,
interchangeable, a world without I,
without distance, perspective or space,
hearts all whole.

The Afterlife

I don't know
              but that our lives,
that is, our everyday lives
in which we breathe,
              and feed ourselves,
and manage the best we can,
are nothing more than one form of afterlife.

What we had lived before must have been a wildness
that no science fiction could approximate.
But then, if this is true,
              what comes after our after,
when death clambers over the wall
and destroys our sweetest contentment?
We imagine wonderful things;
              we watch the infant moon
setting over Mercury, Mars and Venus,
in the afterglow of the sun, and think −
there it is.
              There is our future and our past;
there the dream is prodigal, there
the most fantastic dream is sheltered,
in the sweetness of desire, almost,
              but not quite,
fulfilled.

Lost Ballad

My father gave me water, my mother gave me fear.
In lakes and ocean, in pools I flourished,
but could hear the sorrow stretching,
could feel responsibility's terror.
Oh practical, the song I meant to sing is lost,
buried where my father's temper flared,
hidden from me as it was for them.

My mother gave me books and then was horrified
at what I found. My father never read.
I've eaten everything they gave me,
but hunger led me elsewhere.
Let the hurt be stanched, let their noisy lives
diminish. Then let dogs and cats live deep inside
the way they should, for a son who never sleeps.

Back And Forth

Well, join us, is what I hear.
You've done what you can do.
Why go on? Sleep is your talent now.

Maybe, I think, in the fall light,
the sun warm, the air cool,
maybe, as the spiders die,

and the ivy tendrils work their way
under the shingles of the little house,
maybe that is where I should go.

Maybe I'm done here, having spent
too many hours with the old story,
watching beauty unravel.

It's like music, the same four notes,
a progression into logic. Everyone wants to change;
no one will do it willingly. Not at that cost.

Be concerned only with the real, I've been told.
But who does the defining? Who gets to choose?
Who tells me the heart cannot heal itself,

re-attach the great strings,
snake them into position so they stick,
and are whole again? Who has the nerve

of knowledge, the arrogance of certainty?
Come, it's not too late – there is a finer world.
I am seduced, I am dreaming.
But like my ancestors, I don't know how to go.

2

Above all,
counsel patience.

The man waiting for the deer.
The man waiting for his dream.

That dream waiting to tumble
into the man, who then
refuses what is necessary.

The man who sleeps in leaves.

3
But then, even the smallest voice can change the world.
Though we cannot see, and what is understood
is like the leaves in January wind falling,
something happening you cannot touch
but whose presence is unmistakable. Watching,
though you are a part. Inconceivable,
what gives us a strangeness which is immense,
and much more than we can handle. Go back, then.

Pick the simple things; human relationships
are clearly too difficult. I was working
away from abstraction, a long climb up scree and sand,
where with each step taken, I would slide back,
and after half an hour, I found I was almost
where I had begun. Gasping for breath
at this altitude, heart waking from its sleep;
do I work again, or just quit? and would anyone notice?

4

If I would contain history, which version would I choose?
Never has there been a time when so much
was available and so little known.
Are we at the point where a thousand churches
will again cover the land?
and ignorance is the balm everyone desires?

5

At the first turning of the second stair
I encountered religion, which will not do.
At the second turning of the third stair
I greeted emptiness, a door
that opened out to nothing. I kept on.
At the third turning of the fourth stair
I found the woman in white, the boy
who drowned, the teacher-friend
who lost his mind, the woman
who left, the woman who stayed.
That is how I knew I was home.

6

There is no ending here. I have no Guidance
to tell me where I should be, no matter
how difficult or how certain.
There are no teachers, or rather,
everyone is, which is the same.

I am looking at that great sand mountain,

hundreds of feet above me. I am lugging
a camera, a tripod, certainly water.
The temperature is mild, but soon
I begin to sweat. Sand goes into my shoes;
it is not pleasant. At the summit perhaps
there will be cooling wind. I feel my heart
beating wildly. It is like when I was first in love.
But I know this is different.
This is about my life, what strength I have left.
This is what everyone must do.

After, Or Before

The boat moves swiftly but gently through the still water.
I am on it, watching with little attention the slow swells
the boat makes. There is no land in sight, but this is not an ocean.

I am being taken away but have no idea where or why.
All I know is the sound of water and the faint breeze
that smells like jasmine or lilac.
Whoever else is on this boat stays out of sight,
or perhaps it is just that I don't care and will meet
any companions I have with quiet equanimity.

I realized this winter that there was no paradise,
that my sadness was as close to it as I could get.
Who would wish an emperor's palace
when the soft water makes a faint sound
and the sky is immense with distant clouds,
fire-red from the low sun?
Who would care so much to smash the living world
and all its tenderness just to find, what?
a pure life, a dream? a construction? It is madness.

Better, I think, to watch the molecules drift apart,
form new allegiances.
Because the dead know what we are thinking;
they are spending eternity perfecting themselves,
the thing we would try to do in time,
always, floating on this water,
moving from being the observer of beauty
to the thing itself. I can see it happening.
I brush my hand in the cool water.
It is better than a balm.

I remember the chapparel smell, hiking
on the east side of the mountain,
the sun making oil on the leaves
as we hunted for the one flower
that grew here and only here,
and only at this time of year.
No one could explain this.
No one knew the reason beyond
the reason. It was intoxicating
and that's all that mattered,
that and simply watching
the last green of the flowing grasses
before the real heat began.

Someone had collected God knows how many rocks
and placed them in a single line across the playa
of Panamint Valley. I couldn't see the end,
just one black volcanic stone after another,
stretching into a model of eternity.
We stopped the car, looked at that perfectly straight line,
on both sides of the road and wondered
who could have done it and how.
Not why. That was perfectly obvious.
The rocks were heavy and from a place some distance away.
Someone must have filled a large truck with them,
and slowly carried each rock into the white distance.
Maybe done at night. But not in Summer.
Certainly before the valley had become a National Park.
It lasted a year or two, and then, naturally,
or more likely, deliberately, the rocks
were scattered, or just removed.
These days, when I drive by, I can't decide
whether I want them back or not. But I keep looking.

Not A Criticism

Don't you want to fall in love again?
the old man asked me, almost pleading.
No, I said, wrestling with myself,
I am trying to better the love I have,
not find a new mystery.
For falling in love is ignorance revealed,
the delight of physical pleasure
mixed with the unknown.
Which is not what I care about,
nor barely the beginning of what I do.
It depends whether you think
having your life is a personal matter only,
or a stream in which you are a part.

Square Nails

We are renovating the old, ruined garage.
The first owners knocked out the back
around 1960, so their big fifties Cadillac would fit.
A few years ago, we got rid of the dry rot,
closed off the back, constructed a wall seven feet in, doors,
a new roof and skylight, laid a plywood floor, though tilted,
and finally a level platform for my chair.
It worked, more or less. The Spider Hole, I called it,
because of its many uninvited guests.

Now we are opening up the rest.
The old carpenters used rough-cut redwood 2x3s,
redwood batting for the walls. That wood is priceless now.
I like to think of the builders, ninety years ago,
when this house was one of three on the block
and there were fields all around,
orchards and native grasses which, they tell me,
stayed green the whole year, so that the coastal hills
were not dried out in summer, as they are now.
Then carpenters built this one car garage
that now we are re-modeling,
in our world for our time, as best we can.

I sit early in the morning in my half-finished room.
It is late June and the sun slants through the new north window.
I think of the way language is used to confuse our thoughts,
propaganda everywhere, and thus feel some empathy
with the experimental poets whose work I do not understand.
My way is different, though I think we share intent:
Simple words, simple meanings, clear, direct thought.
Now working with my oldest friend, cool mornings,
the ghosts of the original makers encourage us

to go on, solve the problems, make it clean,
the sweet smell of the cut wood,
and the excellent square cut nails
those first builders used, which I collect and put aside.

The Transition

The pods are about to open – the days of bright flowers are past.
It is time for the swollen seeds to drop and for the plants
to begin their slow dying. We feel it in the air, in the light.
We stand against an inexorable wall, our hearts beating wildly,
fighting the world we are made of, the inevitable repetition
of hope and despair. Worshipping the beauty of the young,
transgressing in so far as we are able, trying to find a solace
in whatever we have gained through time.
We walk just as those before us, humbled,
seeking to find a meaning, or a door, or finally, a respite.

2

I have arrived at the lake. Cradled by a moraine,
with only a few small Lodgepole pines and the twisted,
wind-racked Whitebark. Mostly rocks.
I am tired. The lungs are OK, I'm thinking,
but maybe the heart has been strained more than it should.
I am sweaty, though the heat, at ten thousand feet, is moderate.
I sit down on the duff near the low trees and prop up my pack
with a walking stick to rest, drink water and stare at what is,
for me, eternal. A hummingbird comes by and hovers
a foot in front of my eyes, drawn by the red
of my bandanna, I'm guessing.
I talk to the bird as it moves a few inches to my right,
then a few to my left. I pay attention. Everything is alive
and prescient, everything shimmers like aspen in the wind,
and I, shaking my head, as though in argument,
carry on my objections, my doubts, the separation
I am both delighted by and horrified of.

3

Stones form under tremendous heat and pressure and then,
slowly, are weathered away. This planet will die.
What's beautiful is what's passing, but the act of change
is a constant. The lake's surface is dotted with circles,
fish feeding, insects skimming the water.
I wonder if I should camp here tonight. The whole world
is alive, beating and swirling like my heart.
Nothing is not a constant. There is no nothing.

4

The scientists are wrong. But then, everyone is wrong.
We proceed, fractious and always hungry.
Every day there is a glimpse, whether alone in the high mountains,
or merely in the new room that looks out over the back yard.
It is so hard to see, but finally impossible not to.
Birds are messengers. Stones are as well.
Alpenglow torches the high peaks. It is a fire in the mind.
These are lessons we must learn.
We cannot subvert or outthink the real.
The wheel of the earth is turning, the light changing,
and when the first stars unclothe themselves, it is like the
beginning
of all things. There is a secret calmness to it. So that finally,
Gilgamesh and I are walking through the high country,
mourning our losses, eternally grateful for them.

The Adolescent Of Old Age

I am standing at the western edge of the photograph
watching a naked young man pour water over his head
from the tall, white pitcher he found in the kitchen.
It is warm and the mountains behind are dry
with the smell of herbs. He scrubs himself down
as the older man watches. It is difficult
to remember when he lived here,
washed himself, went into the room with the scent
of oregano and thyme all over his body,
or what it was like every evening
when the sun was shattered by the Plane trees
leading up the walkway, and it stayed warm,
and we ate tomatoes and cucumbers
and cooked orzo and tomato sauce,
and drank the barely drinkable local wine.
I am still in the photograph but beginning to fade,
am drifting into sleep, dreaming of baseball
and trying to remember, in the dream,
what it is I mustn't forget. Because everything
in my life depended on both of these men holding
water in their hands, holding the clear water
as it plashed on the stone porch and quickly dried
in that brilliant sun and caressing air.

A Refusal

Smear, stain, shadow.
The light is dreadful when covered by leaves.
I hear it beating like the thrum of a grouse
in deep words. Thinking furiously, I got to this place
without warning or intent
to find the world bereft of stories.
They had all been told, which meant I had to go.
Or maybe just go my own way.
Even though everyone said I was wrong.
Stain. It felt like that,
arguing was futile. Beating, relentless,
the voice getting hoarse,
as though I'd been shouting half the night.
The gift of age says a friend. *Shadow.*
He means it. Trying to believe against
all evidence. A good task.
Like those nights in Carolina, silent
except for the cicadas and tree frogs
off in the woods beyond the dirt road.
It's a start the voice said. Maybe start over.
Even this late.

Time And Beauty

It seemed there was an eye against the clouds
      the light a prism
of the sun setting behind the last great range
                                 spiked hills
wrenched upwards   thrust in geologic violence
their time   their world
but ours   feet stumbling kicking against rock
breathing heavily
      you realize your body is beginning its farewells

The horses stand in the meadow
          their breath steaming in the early light
moisture off their flanks
two old friends are saying goodbye for the last time
one holds the bridle reluctantly   as if delay could be
permanent
one horse shakes its head   mist rises   the mountains
hidden
where does it go   where does anything go
                    if by movement
we detect a purpose
or are we like the child with a missing chromosome
endlessly walking into the wall
who will never stop until the sad parent leads her gently away

In Perugino's painting, Apollo watches Marsyas play
        the greatest musician of his age
soon he will be flayed by the god for his presumption
      unimaginable agony   was it arrogance
or envy
      yet even the pain
will be a memory and soon not even that
      It is something to look forward to
the water will cleanse us   as we pass into

first element
a continual reworking   re-substance   though
we will never see Perugino again

It is difficult to follow beauty   being there   and then
like a car going by and you standing or better yet
          walking towards it
faces against the window   that you have seen but not known
it is difficult
because if you imitate
                    you digress
they are white those faces
and perhaps there was fear
                    because we are all speeding towards
what   not to beauty   that finds its way regardless
impervious to your pleading   or else it is found simply as a way
ineffably sweet
                    unexpected   and yet striven towards
an unconscious movement of great effort

White face against a curtain
sleeping in the dawn light
                    pillows surrounding her dark hair
the covers tossed around her Sometimes
there is nothing restful about sleep

She ascends a stair
                    turning once to look back
and with a smile while I
                    standing below watch her
grow small
                    ascending to where there is no light
In the dimness she is
standing maybe singing softly to herself
no more than a murmur

Silence Is Imaginary Because The World Never Stops Making Noise.

As the night comes on in the Wachau, a single frog
in the water plants below, astonishingly loud, begins.
He is hesitant, starting and stopping. It seems the whole village
must hear him. He is looking for a mate, but no one answers.
He starts, he pauses, he starts again.

The scientists say that frogs are dying out. No one knows why.
I am sitting on the tiny deck of my hotel room, drinking wine.
How strange and beautiful he is, calling unseen in the darkness,
as the light fades and the mountains reveal a deeper black than
black,
and a soft breeze barely stirs on this warm night.

Jupiter, it must be Jupiter, is the first 'star'. Color is leaving.
The traffic is rare and distant on the river road.
Bells ring every fifteen minutes, two churches
almost in harmony. It is impossible to believe
everything is fading away; the beauty of the earth

cooling before a final consummation with our sun
long after we are gone. Eternity is now,
or rather it has been and will be. We interrupt,
a burglar in the house. We steal whatever is of value;
it affects nothing, a bagatelle. Yet we make eternity

visible. Without us, without the living, without the rocks
and stars, without the lovers in the next room,
nothing is possible. Without the black, or the tentative lights
in this village, without the knowledge we cannot have,
nothing is possible. The wine, as the night, is getting cooler.

The frog is now silent – he has given up – or perhaps
he has other plans, who knows? It is a swirling world,
nothing we do can touch it, and yet it is inside us.
Our bodies praise the bells, in love as we are.
Come, come, there is no distraction, no avoidance;

there is only that magnificent black line which separates
the now darkened sky from the greater dark
of the vineyard mountains and the unseen river beneath them,
that line which continues through the night,
a guidepost to something we will never know.

Chaconne

Who are we to our parent's lives,
that we would describe,
that we would place a marker here
or there, and so define
what we cannot know?
Who were they, considering us
as children – oh if only
our memories were complete,
with nothing lost, so to build
an edifice of the past,
which then is the past
no longer, but a living thing.

If everything we desire is impossible,
then what is the purpose,
why bother with so much
dissatisfaction, when bird
is melded to tree, and to
a white farmhouse
with a weathervane
and the safety of home
that a child sees though the parent
knows better, whatever
the fragmented memory
can hope to find.

I had hoped to bring them back,
to question and discover
what truth there is to discover;
their lives are certain to continue,
as radio waves forever expand,
as our true being, forgotten,

nonetheless continues,
and the suicides also continue,
and our cruelty inexorably builds,
a non-evolutionary history
that learns nothing, growing
not at all, yet returns to where we began.

Finding the yellow shale
in the front yard, near the roses,
and pretending it to be gold,
the immense riches of childhood,
or digging in the lot next door,
black walnut trees and poison oak,
a fort in dirt. It was constant terror
everyday at school for six years,
who could have known?
What are we then perpetuating
if memory fails, if we sit in the sun
in the back yard, and cannot talk?

Is it our dreams that have fashioned
the world? Like the God
in Australia, rising from the mud,
creating everything as he walked
in the empty land, mountains rising,
rivers beginning, all made from mud,
from the thing he was at the beginning,
as we are fashioning a pretend world,
a nightmare, our transient home.
Then we are perfect, our dreams only
failing us, sitting on the great rock
that we made, that is the center.

The Omphalos, a place where
it all began, where memory
mates with knowledge,
where the green seed blossoms
and endlessly dies by beginning
over again, by the glance
from the corner of your eye,
all pressure, all sweetness,
all melded, like it or not. It turns
again, like wind in the desert at night,
hearing the hollow roar of it down
from the mountain, not long before it arrives.

Music

When I die, the part of me that is air
will go into the air. I am air.
When I die, the greater part of me that is water
will go into the streams, the sea. I am water.
When I die, the meat part of me will be consumed;
I will be all animals, all insects; I am devoured
into flesh. I am flesh.
Then what is left will become dirt,
will become rock, will weather and wear away.
I am earth; I am stars, I am being;
there is no emptiness,
there is only taste and savor.

Part 2
Sweet Milk

Transformations

Death is never an option, only an error.
—Ted Hughes: *Tales from Ovid* – Myrrha

1)
It must have seemed to the elderly man that he was running
when the car struck him. So much violence to the body,
so quickly,
                    and he so still.
I looked up in wonder when my parents spoke.
What did it mean they threw a sheet over him?
                What was blood to me, a stain in the middle of the road
that moved from scarlet,
                            to red,
to rust, to dark.

2)
When the two doctors gathered around my mother
to tell her she was dying,
                she nodded yes, she understood,
                            but after a few minutes,
pretended they were just going to take her home,
which, in fact we did.
When I'm walking again,
                        she said to me firmly,
will you teach me how to cook salmon the way you do?

3)
The monks were talking, high up above the cliff,
catching their breaths and trying to figure out
where to build the monastery,
when the young servant following appeared below them
carrying water on the narrow path,

41

                               and slipped,
and fell eight hundred feet out of sight to the rocks below.
The horrified monks were then astonished, fifteen minutes later,
to see him struggling back up the cliff, the pitchers unbroken
and water-filled. It is said angels caught him as he fell,
             and placed him gently on the lower path,
                        so that he must walk up again, in wonder.
             The story says,
similarly,
             that when the authorities finally tired of Paul
             and his obnoxious ranting,
             they beheaded him,
only to discover sweet milk flowed out of his body.

4)
Perhaps I will learn to be grateful,
hear the *amsel* singing as I walk among the trees
in the gathering mist.
                   The horses are disturbed by the quiet.
Their breath makes spirits in the chill morning air.
They are impatient to be going, snorting and pawing the ground.
The aspen are beginning to turn and the clear, sharp air
drives through the ponderosa while I get ready.

A Doppler Shift

Sometimes, when we're making love,
        I know there are two other people,
who lend their bodies to us,
        who lend, even, their sensations,
so that we can understand how it feels
        to be human. I think, perhaps,
        that we are not,
or that being human is a phase. Our small cries are guideposts
that we make, but cannot read.

Get it done with, get it done with,
I said silently to my mother as she died.
        Not said with impatience; rather
wanting to fast forward the time,
        to be finished,
because this part was dreary, and I'd stretch my back in its stiffness
and look at the days before us,
        long, or maybe not.
To get through a thing because it is not real
        to me, or being real,
distracts my sense of possibility. Making love
is not a fantasy, but I begin to question
        where one thing ends
and another begins. Who is the lover, who beloved?
        I am as borrowed, and the time of it
is neither my own, nor substantial.
        The wind carries in the coolness
from the ocean as I walk in the hills. I am unable,
        or unwilling, to ask
the moment to stay.
        But if I do, and when I can,
it will be like grinding cardamom and fennel seeds together –
the perfume will be even better than the taste.

Von Ewiger Liebe

The man sat out in the garden looking vaguely up,
half listening to the birds. He was fiddling with twigs
and an acorn, and didn't notice when I approached.
I called to him softly and he seemed to recognize my voice.
He said the Spirits were singing
and I mustn't make any loud noises or move suddenly.
I had just come from his wife,
who, the doctors said, was not allowed to visit.
It would upset him too much, they said.
She had held me before I left, eyes averted.
That day I realized he would not get better,
would slowly drift away into that other, maybe finer world,
and leave her finally to me. Leave us together.
I have never been so terrified in my life.

Siegmund In The Desert Without Protection

1

Tony said it must have been fear
that made me want to go back early.
We had been in the dunes almost a week.
No one had come by. Only once had we seen, miles away,
a campfire at night. Someone was out there, had come over
the rocky pass to the north, and camped. Gone the next day
even though I panned the area over and over with my binoculars.
Maybe, in the silence, when there was only desert, wind,
and the occasional bird, gray and faint, calling
distantly out by the rocks before the sun came up,
maybe I realized just how empty I was.
And, after photographing every day pictures
which I laughingly described as *photographs of nothing*,
it began to be real, that nothingness, and the knowledge
it was all I had. That's when I wanted to go.

2

I watched the train as it lumbered out of the *Gare du Nord*
and wondered what I would do without her.
We would meet, I hoped, in a couple of weeks in Beaune,
but I thought I might lose her to Germany once she had returned,
not knowing whether I could manage in France alone,
too afraid to go into the Boulangerie to order a baguette,
thinking the world might crush me, leave me
helpless, a man unable to speak.
I feared the great world outside was just as hostile
as the indifferent wilderness.
I could find no ease in either.

3

We found the cabin at the end of a rugged dirt road
at the head of a canyon. There was still snow
on the protected north-facing slopes. There were a few piñon pines
by the dry stream bed, otherwise just mesquite, and gray
bitterbrush.
Behind, the mountains, bare and silent, cut off the view.
No one lived in the cabin, and it wasn't locked.
It was clean, had a wood burning stove on one side,
a mattress on the other, and a small table in front of the one
window
that looked down the canyon to the distant valley thirty miles
away.
You could write in the book on the table, or cook,
using the few utensils that had been left in the kitchen area.
What must it be like living there?
I would have liked to stay, with my small kerosene lamp
and a decent supply of food, watching the light in its steady
progress
across the valley, talking to no one, watching, being quiet,
finding the spring up the canyon behind the cabin
and fetching enough water to manage;
listening to the occasional birds which believed that,
in this vast and empty landscape a mate could be found,
listening, without expectation yet attentive, without hope
but nonetheless prepared for that one particular pattern of sound
that meant there was a purpose,
a god that watched over these proceedings, guided, leant meaning
to the huge space that otherwise, in spite of its beauty, said only
I am empty, I am alone.

Thinking that when Hunding came and his sword
entered my body and the last thing I saw was not Wotan grieving,
rather the pervious desert, accepting my blood as it flowed
through my hands into the dry soil, drinking me to renew itself,
taking my body as part of itself, until I learned at last
there was no difference, there was only sun, eyes,
and the breathing that contained all the sorrow in the world.

The Achieved

1

He wakes, hearing cries in the dark. He wonders
what animal it could be, as though it were injured, or lost,
or surrounded by something terrifying.
It rends his heart. He feels he knows exactly
that the animal is speaking his words.

The woman has heard them too, and sits up. *What is it?*
she says. *I don't know.* As the sounds cease, she settles
back down close to him and, after a time, falls asleep.
They are protected by their long knowledge of each other
the way a tent protects you in the desert;
it feels much more than it is.

Still, he gets up after about an hour and looks out
in the early morning, overcast light, not seeing anything,
wondering what it would be like on his own, alone with his grief,
which unaccountably now fills his whole body,
as complete as an orgasm, tears as he grips the table,
looking out to the silent yard –
Has love brought me here? he says softly,
not wanting to disturb anything. *I should add them up,*
what I have, what I am missing, what there is to find,
and where it leads. Is grief better than happiness?
He feels something in him leaking out which the cries announce.

2

Two days later it is as if nothing has happened.
As though he'd forgotten, as though he could forget,
and live his life, busy in the days – though the nights wander back,
and he cannot rid himself each morning of a sense of loss.

Sometimes searching his pockets, or wandering in the house,
rubbing a sore back, thinking it was something
almost remembered, almost known. Sitting down,
almost confused and a little weary, asking his animal for help.

That night he watches the movie again, just the last scene,
where the man, sobbing and silent, carries her out of the cave
into the fierce sun. *Is something missing from my life,*
he asks, *or is it just hunger?* lost in his own tears then,
unable to explain, only knowing this is serious,
and must not be forgotten.

3

That night she dreams they are flooding *Chartres* with great
pumps.
The water wears off the gold, ruins the tapestries;
the windows explode from the pressure; water is streaming out
through the widening cracks;
soon there will be nothing but rubble.
She is weeping out in the fields.

We are taking a train in twilight. The twilight is permanent.
Sullen black houses stand one on one;
smoke and shadowy figures are seen in the faint light.
A hint of burnt green where grass should be.

She murmurs in the bed until I wake and hold her,
telling her softly it cannot be.
Even though we doubt all our lives,
fearing what little order we've made
shortly will be swept away.
The dark figures pull at us,

emptying our achievements.
I tell her, I tell myself; it is the best I can do.
In the morning the animals are still,
hiding somewhere beyond what we know.

Homeless Man In The Mission District

The man was walking slowly along the street
with his arms raised, as though acknowledging applause.
This man's audience must have been pleased.
He had great dignity there as he slowly made his way,
turning a little, wanting to include everyone in his triumph.
People looked at him briefly and looked away.
Or avoided him entirely by crossing the street
well before he passed. He did not speak.
I thought of Delphi and the victorious Charioteer,
the young man of black bronze staring straight ahead,
a fixed look of both pride and modesty
as he held the invisible reins to the now lost chariot and horses,
to circle the stadium once again and forever in his victory.
The real world not seen, not analyzed, not reduced,
but surely there, prepared for our acknowledgment,
our modest assent as we flicker in and out,
pretending what we know to be the only world,
pretending in our ignorance not to see,
and then believing what we make,
constructing the lesser thing to obscure the magnificent.

Mentês

Odyssey, Book 1, lines 121 - 366

How do I know the God is speaking and not the man?
that one friend is wise, or that other
knows what he is about? Given his own life,
can I trust what he says about mine?
Where is the God in all this? Where the rustle
of unseen clothing, the wind with sound but no movement?
where is the animal breathing though there is no animal?
I want the signs as they have always been to guide me,
but must reinvent them, because the God now
jumps from one sign to another, from the confused man
who cannot see himself clearly but, for a moment,
sees something in me, to the cat at dusk who waits
near the top of the hill, and then flops on his back
with a little sound of pleasure as I approach, and then runs away,
to the fog opening, revealing the one oak on the hillside,
and then swiftly closes down again.
What I find is seen at the edge of sight, and not clearly.
I am hungering for Mentês, for a reliable guide,
who will lead me inexorably to my father,
or the clear movement that will make my life a still pool,
bordered by the clean granite. That will not so much
ease the suffering, as help it bear fruit.

The Work

I am working in two bare rooms with unpainted walls
and covered-over windows out in the industrial section of town.
I look at invoices, find the bottles, put them in cases
and check them off, then seal and stack the boxes.
I try not to make the mistakes I always make
no matter how careful I am. The tiny radio
sits on a stack of three cases and plays Brahms.
The sound is poor, but I can imagine the whole orchestra,
and fill in the parts I know but don't actually hear. I bend over,
lift the heavy cases, move them around, use a knife to pry open
the new ones, then put the knife back in my jacket pocket,
making sure I have the right wine. Sometimes I stop
and sit in the one chair for a moment, drink water
from a plastic bottle and wonder what on earth I'm doing
with my life. Whether I actually like it or not,
whether I enjoy this thing I have created to help me live in the
world.
I sit and think and listen to the music and cool down a little
before getting up again, stretching my back, getting the stiffness
out.
Maybe I should put prints on the walls. Put a table in one corner.
Maybe soften the austerity. I work on until it begins to get dark.

Further Instructions

This difficult day, like the others,
could teach me one good thing,
were I ready to receive it.
As when I bit my tongue so firmly
that I felt a crunch before the pain,
and the salt flowed freely in my mouth,
and I winced and tried to find something
to cauterize the wound, or forget, or just
put my mind on something else, as though
that were the point of the exercise, not the real point,
not the lesson, not the gift.
Because what we do to ourselves
is a kind of gift, in that we presume
a greater knowledge than we have,
and I am walking through the house whimpering,
furious at my own carelessness,
at my inability to live as a god lives,
as Apollo standing serenely in that painting –
at least as I picture him – not above it all,
but confident in his mastery. The way I am not.
As the throbbing decreases, I think:
Pay attention. It is the only lesson I need to know.

The Perfect Cat

*...das freie Tier hat seinen Untergang stets hinter sich und vor
sich Gott, und wenn es geht, so gehts in Ewigkeit
(The free animal has its decline behind it, and before it God, so
that when it moves, it moves, and lives, in eternity)*
—Rilke, *8th Duino Elegy*

Sometimes I'd wake in the middle of the night
from a noise the house has made, and then hear her
clawing her way up onto the bed (she was always
a poor jumper) to settle herself on the pillow I have placed
next to mine, where she liked to sleep, and where later she died.
When I water the azalea, I hope she is content in her dreaming.
The Indians believe that cows come back as human beings,
maybe even wise people. But I believe cats were human already,
often many times – they come back to enjoy themselves
completely,
and, if we are attentive, show us how to be happy.
It could be. I have a photo of a monk, standing,
shaved head and robe with funny striped pants
showing at the bottom, his eyes closed in apparent meditation,
standing alone in a bare, open space with dark, blurry trees behind.
His arms are crossed in front of his body,
cradling a cat on its back, the two rear feet
poised high up, the tail in between, the front paws
comically crossed over, the head turned towards the camera,
eyes most interested and bright, staring at the photographer,
and us. A whisper of a smile is on the monk's face,
and on the cat's perhaps a little pride,
as though it had just consumed the best part of a chicken.
At the very least, a knowledge in that black and white face,
that totally sprawled body, relaxed and trusting,
that it had got precisely what it wanted, and was content.

Rejecting The Evidence

It happened just the other day. I bent down
to pick up a smooth, river-rounded stone
and then idly threw it down the trail.
But the act of throwing was painful.
The rock landed maybe thirty feet away,
and I, shocked at my own weakness,
held my aching arm and wondered what was wrong.
I tried it again, and then again, then side-armed the throw.
But it was no good. I had become feeble.
I stopped, put my jacket down, and got serious.
Started practicing, trying to build up strength,
trying to find a way that wasn't so painful,
measuring the distance in paces after each toss.
Worked at it for maybe half an hour.

Picture a man in his fifties, standing alone in a valley,
with the brown September hills silent around him,
throwing rocks like a little boy, throwing,
overhand, submarine, winding up like a pitcher
and throwing, and pacing, and coming back,
sometimes gripping his arm in pain,
triumphant at forty steps, miserable at twenty,
trying to prove he was not getting old.

Something Better Than Hope

Let him keep singing, he said,
and thought the practice might help, later,
when the singing stopped.

Let him do as he must,
let him change as he will,
let the sorrows that make beauty
overwhelm him,
let him go through,

he said, more to himself
than to anyone who might hear.
The repetition will bear
fruit, let me suffer
for him,

      that there may be
movement, as a star moves,
as the emptiness is filled
with more emptiness,
which is what the singing
prevented,
and made.

Part 3
The Time Between Worlds

A Different Season

The earth is cooling this November evening.
The first grasses are already inches high,
and the dark ground has begun to push itself up,
tilting the flagstones in the back. Roots are moving.
The spiders, so numerous and fat in their grand webs
two weeks ago, are gone, their remnant architectures
breaking apart. It is the time between worlds,
where dry, wind-blown leaves are a distant music.
I know it comes around again, but must resist
the temptation; we will not be part of that return.
After the phone call with her slowly dying mother,
Jane says wearily, as she undresses and joins me in bed:
*I'm beginning to think we are just organisms,
nothing more.* And reaches over to turn out the light.

The Pull

I wake in my parent's house, put on shorts and a t-shirt
and walk down the hallway into the living room.
By the Queen Anne table next to the big couch,
I pick up a pewter cup, and note how dusty it is.
No one seems at home, so I look out the big window
to the flagstone porch, the maple tree
with faded leaves that has never been healthy,
and the entire San Fernando Valley spread out
down the hill, with the big mountains behind.
It is then I realize that everyone is dead,
the house long ago sold and remodeled.
I am thinking how these dead people still dictate
their will to us, and how much effort it takes
to find our way through them into our own lives.

Celebration

Water is pouring off the roof corner
hard onto the cement below.
The drain must be clogged with leaves.
One thunderstorm has passed
but the wind has picked up
and another is on its way.
Off in the distance, sirens.
In the space between storms
I can hear the neighbor's power saw
as he works on his cottage.
The cat jumps up, settles on my chest,
his eyes on my eyes until both, slowly,
close. There is only the sound of water
and the smell of the drying Christmas tree.
My back hurts from the fall yesterday
going down the steps to the flooded basement.
The slight pain of pressure now
from the cat's weight is strangely comforting.
In the darkening room it seems foolish to move,
so I find myself thinking of a friend
who writes that he cannot imagine
an artist of yes in our time.
Right now, half dozing, half dreaming,
I'm certain he's wrong.

A Summer Spent Reading Chekhov

The store front faced northeast, so that, in the long, hot afternoons,
the light seemed to drain out and across the street
to the white facades of the other stores.
Traffic was constant, the flashing of sun
on the big trucks' windows making me look up
as they rumbled past. Inside, everything was quiet,
the chairs and tables in their dark mahogany,
the Ralph Earls and other Primitives on the walls,
wrought iron and old cut glass and colonial snuff boxes –
even grandfather clocks not ticking.
All that Summer I sat in the back and read,
and got up maybe twice or three times a day
to answer questions from the few stray customers who came in.
Mostly I peopled the store with the young officer
kissed by accident, or the woman who discovers how tempting
an affair with the lawyer would be, or the suicide.
They fit so splendidly among the 18th and 19th Century pieces.
Beyond, along Ventura Boulevard and the palm and eucalyptus,
they were as lost and out of place as I was.

Different, Not Alien

It is easy to recognize the boy, who, trying to time his arrival
at the class down the hill to be almost, but not quite late,
and could therefore walk into the back of the classroom
relatively unnoticed, arriving earlier than he wished,
watching with horror as the tough boy charged up the knoll,
and the others from below laughing and calling out
his name, and, aiming directly towards him, he frozen
almost in disbelief as the other closed and then,
lowering his shoulder, crashed into him, knocking him to the
ground,
his books flying in the air, papers scattering in the light wind,
not hurt exactly, but his uniform covered with grass stains,
getting up slowly while the other turned and strode back
to his friends and their appreciative cheers, he standing finally,
collecting his things, and making his way down, alone,
to the classroom, arriving late, and the rest of the class smirking,
whispering among themselves, the teacher arriving,
maybe understanding what had occurred, but not really
able to do much about it, maybe not wanting to either,
the boy sitting down, completely alone, but not alien,
knowing somewhere the meanness in himself, knowing
but unable to say it, that were there someone
stranger still, someone to bring out their fears even more
than he did, perhaps he would be in that small crowd as well,
laughing and jeering, coming of age, learning
the rules everyone pretends are normal, and true.

Mr. Truman Declares War – Probably

The radio sound was bad, but you could still hear
that flat, Midwestern voice. Whatever he was saying
must have been important, though I remember none of that.
Just that my parents had stopped whatever they were doing
to listen, and the shellacked knotty pine walls
of the cabin, dark and almost sticky,
and the smell of pines, and the lake.
We were swimming in it – I had newly learned how.
We also fished: small, silver, flat fish
my mother fried for dinner. It was paradise.
That other world hardly existed, until one day I heard
that someone named Senator Taft had died,
and I didn't know what it meant,
except I did somehow, and even though my parents
and then my grandmother told me fantastic stories
to explain away my questions and my fears,
I knew they were not true.
But in the time before that,
there were only mountains and the sound of the great trees
moving in the wind, and the water, and the three of us.
I am certain we were happy, and I went to bed
tired and content, secure in the knowledge that next day,
and the one after, I would again be in the magical wild.

Wasting Time

I fear it draining out of me but am not moved
to do anything. Somehow, fifty years have passed
and I am still the boy standing after school by the gym
in the weak winter light waiting for his mother to come.
I keep planning to build that cabin in the desert,
or the mountains, or the Austrian countryside,
so I can do nothing in particular – listen to music
perhaps, read something, drink good wine.
The ambition remains but only out of oddity.
What use has the world for it?
You can squeeze a person indefinitely,
but what does the crop yield?
Who is the ghost standing in the back yard
by the clothesline that keeps whispering,
but just loud enough so that I can hear
through the neighbor's television, the distant traffic,
and the sound of conversation in the spring nights:
hurry, hurry, loss is only make believe.
You have no time you can do everything you ever wanted.
But what, I keep asking, if I have no idea,
and all possibilities seem equally defensible,
and it goes through my fingers anyway?

Learning From The Master

I am at my desk, half-asleep in the late afternoon.
The summer sun comes through the two windows
and the open door, lies on my desk and the other chair
where the cat sleeps. We are very quiet.
Only a faint breeze in the leaves
and the humming of the computer,
which I cease hearing after a few minutes.
I think: *I am getting old*, as my eyes droop
and the yellow desk shimmers.
But nothing's changed, I answer back.
The shell of me alters; the core remains.
Right, I hear, *and when the core of you dies,*
what then? I murmur a little, and shift in my chair,
trying to get comfortable, wishing there were something
to rest my head against. Myshkin is quite asleep,
his paws tucked under, perfect and silent.
A spider hangs from the window, light flowing through his body
as though it were made of glass.
I don't want to answer.
The phone rings, and I get up, cross the yard and listen
to the message, which is in German, but not for me.
I sit back down, knowing I must stop soon, and make dinner.
But it is so lovely here, in deep summer, arguing faintly
with the truth, determined to have it both ways.

Mortality

The dinner was perfect: sand dabs sautéed in olive oil with cumin,
Swiss chard with garlic, tiny artichokes, rice, and a light sauce,
everything fresh, organic, and well prepared.
Towards the end of the meal, Jane, looking down at her plate,
wondered aloud *"What would be the best final bite,*
What should I eat last?"

Ways Of Deceit

By now, I must know all the tricks:
simple avoidance as well as
the more elaborate plots of self-deception.
I know the tone that initiates,
between us, an agreement.
         And my knowledge implies consent,
a co-conspiracy laughter when nothing is funny
to smooth the moment - a transition piece
away from the emptiness or the pain. Don't show anything,
the story goes; or something worse than death
follows.
         For instance, when my Father
broke down at the kitchen sink after dinner
while Mother wandered through the house muttering
to her visions, at God, at cats, at the dark window
open to the night; he speaking, finally,
to me, after thirty-seven years, something which,
because of the flood of tears and the water running,
I could not clearly hear, about other women, and his love
of my mother, and his growing helplessness – And I not knowing
what to do, standing there awkwardly, with a towel and a plate,
wishing I could ask him to repeat, explain,
be clear, once and for all.

Without Order

I have preserved the night,
kept him in my tent,
sang the sweet song of growing old,
counting as though there were truth
in what I did. Sometimes it seems
like forever; sometimes,
as my father said, or warned,
it is no time at all,
a shadow in a glass.
Oh wait, wait, it will soon be over,
over as in the impossible
ending – a mother dies, a father,
quick, quick, let it be finished,
let something else
be. If something else is,
if singing merely
can make it so.

I keep the night close to me,
keep metal in the mouth
as protocol, as the smiling man
who has no order within
and knows there will never
be, or need be,
because what is known is
not enough, and being not enough
only assures us what is missing.
In the tent the lack
comforts me.

It is the only comfort I have,
or need. I am watching my life
in water – I am hearing
what we are all given to hear,
as though that form were real,
as though we could envision
what we are.

Grief Reworked

Lump of flesh stuffed into a black bag,
hauled out through the garage,
put in the van, and taken away.
Frankly, I've had it with death.
But she looked like a young girl,
head to the side, mouth slightly open,
dreaming, it seemed, when I came in.

Now, more than five years later,
I think of her as I never knew her,
a young woman in some
Los Angeles nightclub,
slightly shrinking from the camera,
but elbow firmly on the table,
cigarette held up and burning.
Her new husband is next to her,
in a dark suit, smoking.
It could be Turner and Garfield.
You know they're going to be trouble.

I cannot see either of them
as I knew them. Yes,
the sea breaks over their bodies,
washing everything away.
The real is insufficient to the true.
The medieval mind got that part of it right;
we are cleansed on our way to paradise.
But that goes for everybody,
not just the saved. There are no damned.
There was never any choice,
only fable to help us,
or the human story, to distract us.

To understand the true, Nietzsche said,
you must look out of the corner of your eye,
and see only the periphery.
Which is why knowledge,
though useful, is not enough.
My mother, in a sun dress,
walks purposefully
through the Southern California light.
My father is with her, though
it seems he is following. So are
the animals, and her mother.
They are going some place
together again, but because
the goodbyes I made
were permanent,
I will not be with them.

Going Home

We meet at the roadside cafe and I sit facing the window.
The cars go by and the donut shop across the road is busy
with unhealthy-looking people going in and out.
We are the only ones here, except for the cook and owner.
My cousin and I talk about the old times.
He is older and knows more about my family than I do.

Is it really true that my mother and grandmother
broke into my great uncle's office the night he died,
and took what they thought was valuable,
because they knew they would be left out of the will,
fairly or unfairly? My cousin describes all this
without passion and with sympathy for these dead people.

His hair is white, mine, mysteriously, not.
We are the last of our family. The food here is good,
the atmosphere warm. It has an old feel about it,
and the owner refills our cups and talks with us.
I love his loud Hawaiian shirt, and the fact
that he will sometimes trade food for wine.
It is like the past in Los Angeles,
where we knew everyone, and everyone had a secret,
and they all lied, and the world was orderly and secure.

Guilty

Other than the usual humiliations of Grammar School
I remember very little, but I do remember one recess.
With an empty soft drink bottle in my hand,
I was called somewhere, and tossed the bottle softly
but not accurately to the sandbox a few feet away
and missed high, hitting the metal bar bells.
The glass shattered, and a teacher came by
at just that moment. My punishment was harsh.
He held me by the ear, twisted it, and marched me
in pain and tears to my classroom. Stood me
in front of the class to confess my crime.
Though, as I remember, it was still recess
and the class, unruly and noisy, and really
not paying much attention to me at all,
barely noticed the terrified boy in front of them.
The rest drifts back into lost memory.
It was just a scene, though I can still see that bottle
lazily twisting through the air, to my horror
not where I aimed it, but on its own willful way,
smashing and glittering into the bright sand.

Claustrophobia

After dinner, my father lay down on the blue love seat,
his legs overhanging one arm,
head resting uncomfortably on the other.
My mother sat stiffly on the opposite love seat,
facing him across a table with a large silver bowl on it,
filled with imitation fruit. I was in one of the wing chairs
off to the side, just back from college, and now living
400 miles north. We would try and make conversation.
The big, formal living room with its precisely placed furniture
and severe, 18th Century paintings made it difficult.

One evening, I let slip something about poetry,
and my Father scrunched himself up
to a half-sitting position, so he could see me better.
With an edge to his voice, asked *What's the angle?*
my Father who, to the best of my knowledge,
never read a book in his life, or a poem,
only the newspaper where he worked.
Though he was angry, I think he genuinely wanted to know.
He thought there must be some trick that would make sense.
But I had no tricks. He must have felt completely shut out
by his son. And had I known what to reply,
how could I have said it, and to what end?
What do you do when your children baffle you?
In the last years, I think he just gave me up for lost,
and spent what energy he had trying to protect my mother.
As he had always done.

I lie on that same couch in the late afternoon,
in another city, in another life, thinking
of all the questions we never asked each other

and of the few answers we unsatisfyingly gave.
They hang in the air forty years on.
Breathing them, I feel like my mother felt
when she was dying of emphysema,
trying as hard as I can to breathe,
but with only the used-up dead air of all our sorrows
and misunderstandings with which to work.

Part 4
Learning To Breathe Again

First Night In The Desert

Trying to remember how to put up the tent.
The wind making it difficult, everything flapping
as I flop down on it, spread-eagled, pounding each stake
with a rock, relearning what will become automatic
in three days. Blowing up the air mattress.
Putting books, flashlight and paper next to the sleeping bag.
Cutting onions and potatoes. Opening the wine.
Peeling and adding garlic. Smelling my hands with pleasure.
Turning on the little light that makes intimate the two tables
in the huge twilight. Beginning to forget everything
that, twenty-four hours ago, seemed important.
Adjusting to a different scale of time.

Feeling the expected fear rise up in me as the light fades
from the last clouds to the west. Looking east
to the deep purple, and black outlines of mountains.
The wind quieting. Letting the fear leak out
beyond the little pool of light into the darkness.
Respecting it, but not letting its size imply strength.
Standing in the dark, peeing. Standing out there
longer than necessary. Learning to breathe again.

Definition In The Desert

I turned on the radio this morning
after a quiet, cold night in the Greenwater valley.
My thermometer read 26°, but it felt fine.
Probably no one around me
for thirty miles in any direction.
One coyote song before the sun, nothing else,
though the faint high-pitched calls
of Horned Larks flying had awakened me.

They were playing music of Handel,
and the woman introduced the piece
by saying he was a master of dignified grief,
which his contemporary audience demanded.
I put my small camera on the freezing tripod
and tried again to photograph the dawn.

Not Sleeping Much

What lasts? I said to the moon,
just rising for the last time over the bare ridge
in the early dawn. *Does the I last?*
But the moon was having none of it, and was silent.
Then a short warm gust of wind
from the dunes to the west said: *No. The I*
is not real, is merely the pattern a shrub makes
on sand in the wind. It comes, it goes—it
may be beautiful but you are not it.
I turn back east again, tired, unable to sleep,
pulling up the sleeping bag to protect myself—
If these ridges in starlight are not real, why
should I care about what is? These things we have:
the scorpion I found crushed under the tarp,
the pain in my back as the long night concludes,
the first bird's call just before color returns.
Maybe that's enough.

Singing With Annie In The Panamint Valley

After setting up camp, I made and ate a simple dinner,
sat inside the car to listen to music.
One song, whose words I knew,
on the possible comforts in death, moved me deeply.
Hearing it now, I got outside the car, and with the volume up,
sang myself, who would never sing in front of others,
sang in this great valley with not another person in ten miles,
in the silence, singing to death
as though he could be encompassed by our voices.

Rhapsody: Full Moon Over The Ibex Dunes

After our deaths, we become the emptiness
that shapes the earth, the moon, the stars.
We make the circle shape of them;
we are the inside that allows light
to burst out of its space; we are the element
that gives being purchase.

The moon rises over the dark mountains
and their alluvial plains, and the sand dunes rest,
free of wind on this one cloudless night.
My tent mesh is open on both sides and above,
the moon rising steadily –
if only we could be protected –
assured that this life was the right one,
that all our motion worked together, being, non-being –
and that we could not distinguish between the two.

Tell me how much will be needed.
What will it take for a life well lived?
What will it take for the pain, like fire or its fuel,
to consume, or be consumed?

After A Day Photographing In The Desert

Eyes burning from the glare, I got back to the campsite,
put the tripod down and hung my pack on it,
peeled off all my clothes, and, dripping with sweat,
poured about a quart of water over my head,
soaked the bandanna with a little more, and scrubbed myself down.
Let the air dry me, standing sore-footed on rocks,
blinking in the late afternoon sun. Reached in the car
to the ice box, pulled out a beer, and, sitting on the tailgate, naked,
drank it, putting the cold bottle against my forehead.
When the sun went behind the bare slope behind me,
I put on clean clothes, and a jacket, got out the camp chair,
facing the great valley I had just crossed,
and watched, thinking of nothing, listening to nothing.
What more could I possibly want? I kept wondering.
What is there in this that finalizes all desire?

Sudden Wind And Storm Under The Panamints

Leaning against the car, protecting ourselves against a fierce wind,
the night coming on, a few drops stinging our faces
and the sand blowing hard out in the valley.

My tent pole had snapped in the wind, and I wondered
how this trip would work now, thinking yet another thing
had gone wrong, and I'd have to return home, defeated.
But later that night, the clouds cleared,
and the incredible stars poured out.

Unable to sleep, I watched them through the mesh
in their stately pavane, gradually circling, horizon to horizon.
The wind slowly died, the silence took over, and I finally slept.

In the morning, a roaring stove, hot tea together,
and we could believe in something again.
Light on the distant sand dunes, the creosote bushes
in their exquisite patterns across the valley.

The Panamint Valley

What could be better than waking in the pre-dawn,
a faint brightness over the dark peaks to the east,
the air alive, almost stirring, but not a sound anywhere?

Then getting up in the dark, lighting the camp stove,
boiling water for tea, holding the steaming cup in both hands,
and talking slowly with a friend as the moon slips below
the western slopes, the down jacket snug around my neck.

Slowly, the tent takes on color, its blue against the salt flats,
like a strange ship in the vastness of water. Slowly,
as everything brightens here, the rest of the world
falls away, is taken by the first crows circling,
and lost as the sun turns rock to purple, and then red.

I know that when the great wind finally rises,
and comes to blow the dried husk of me away,
to be scattered once again, changed into air and rock and tree,
I will not remember the things we built;
only the things we are.

The Perfume Of Mountains

When the birthday came that was a signature of old age,
I felt, like everyone else, no different.
It was just another lousy number without meaning.
Except it wasn't.

A few days later I'm sitting on the deck of a cabin
high up in the Sierra, surrounded by Jeffrey Pines.
Walking up to Granite Lake with a friend yesterday,
I realize I will probably never backpack again.

A four mile hike with a five hundred foot gain
in altitude is plenty, which used to be nothing.
The body I carry no longer seems a part of me
it is all of me.

Linda wrote that the pleasure of just lying in the Aegean sun
can, at least for a time, overcome all the misery of the world.
Yes, you do need to be young to believe that;
otherwise, it sounds almost immoral.

But sitting here in the sun and vanilla scent of the pines,
feeding the Steller Jays out of my hand,
is almost enough to make me forget
that women no longer look at me the way they used to.

Inyo

What if the Great Spirit resides, not on Chomolungma, or
Olympus,
or the summit of Aconcagua, or Denali, or even in the rugged Inyo,
and those other desert mountains I spend so much time in,
dwells, not in those wild places especially,

but is instead camped in my little room, once a one-car garage,
then a ruin, now, after seven years, finally converted,
a part of it at least, into my study.
What if the Great Spirit has moved into a small space
in Berkeley, with its severely sloped floor
and side window that will not completely shut,

my Inyo, my dwelling place, uncertain in the first rain,
without heat, but a home nonetheless.

I must be careful here, I think, watching a tiny spider
make its web in the corner of a dirty window pane.
What could be so much smaller than it
that it could catch there, that it could feed and prosper?

Traveling Man

When a woman gets the blues,
she hangs her little head and cries.
But when a man gets the blues,
he grabs himself a train and rides.
—Jimmy Rogers

I drove into the silent valley where there is no shade,
still hearing the engine of my mother's breathing machine.
It thrummed and groaned and gurgled endlessly.

At night, I wanted to go down the stairs
and pull the plug, so there could be silence,
so she could die in silence, beyond quiet
and a battered body, and the gasping for air.

So I left. Drove eight hours out to the center of the valley.
Set up camp and watched the shadows move
across the Argus Range to the Panamints,
the mountains becoming blacker than the night.
Watched also the wind pause, and stutter, and flicker out,
then stars in the moving air above and the night around me.

But the machine kept pumping. It went on and on,
under the sky, under God, whose bright silence
is never distracted – though I am.

It surged inside me, my own heart beating, my blood,
the breath I take, here, in the open, as though
I could somehow replace that stinking dark room
with five planets in alignment, and a late moon,
and a son traveling, perhaps blindly, beyond the world's curve.

With Only The Sound Of Wind Accompanying

The Marsh Hawk starts up and flies across the open field;
the coyote trots off purposefully but in no hurry,
its head turning back occasionally to watch
as you approach. Even the cows avoid you,
jerk back and look alarmed when you stop and speak to them.
Though surely it is a mistake to equate wildness with fear.
Or that what you see in those gray unblinking eyes is alien.

When the hawk tilted in the air, she seemed to ride
far out to the west, over the ridge, and then back,
dipping under the current to find her way
to the bare branch that hardly stirred when she landed,
folded her wings under, and stilled.
We call that motion Grace because there is nothing in it
that has to do with you as separate or alone.

Anywhere In The World

I walk back down the valley in early evening light.
Wanting it to last, I go slowly, looking up at the rounded,
grass-covered hills, and their dark folds thick with oak.
I get to a large clearing and the pen where two hundred goats
are quieting for the night. They see me and turn towards me,
watching with their mad hourglass eyes while I stop to watch them.
A few grunt and fart and make a sound like shuffling in the dirt.
Far off, up where the trees are, a Great-Horned Owl
calls, slowly and luxuriantly. My eyes half-close
in the chill air while the last sun gleams
on the grassy summits five hundred feet above.
Then continue down the path.

The Odd Comfort In Not Living Long Enough

I come back to the pond, and, finally, it is dry.
I have watched for six months as it rose and then subsided,
slowly, the reeds growing steadily towards the middle,
the frogs leaping into the center when I come near.
It lies in a fold at the end of the narrow valley.
From it, the trail goes up steeply to the ridge
and the flat place I would build a house on if it were allowed.
I would build up close to the oak, but still in the clear,
looking to the east, knowing, if I had a garden,
the deer would come out of those woods behind
and devour everything. And I'd work to keep them out.
Last week the pond was down to six feet across
and only inches deep. I thought maybe the rains
would come soon and fill it before it was gone.
Like the way our lives end just before we are reborn.
So that we cannot know how it happens,
how our home is made ready for us.
And that, when it seems we have lost everything,
the rains do not come; instead, there is more light,
a smoky dryness and the clicking of empty stalks
rubbing against each other when the wind finds them,
deep in the quiet valley, at the center of our lives.

California Doppelgänger

My living ghost walks with me in the Briones hills
east of Berkeley. The morning fog hangs, still thick,
in the valleys and on the ridges, so that when I hear him,
it is a sound that carries through the dense silence
of early morning. I stop, and turn around, several times,
forgetting he is not of our world and, of course, cannot be seen.
But why does he kick pebbles as I do?
Why does he make the wind rustle and breathe, the way I do,
if he is not one of us, and, in fact, whose presence
is a kind of rebuke to me, which says that my world is insufficient.
Why does he use the world at all, crush plants,
release the herbal scent around me, as I do?
This place is mine, not his. These rocks, grasses, poison oak,
California Laurel, red-tailed hawk, and the fore-leg of a deer
I found on the trail. What is eaten here is mine. What is torn apart,
dragged into the deep brush, has nothing at all to do with him.
I am the wine of the world, the crushed juice of the earth,
the fragrance of time. I am dry, I am sweet, I flow into the waters
of our beautiful planet. This is my time, not his, who has no time.
I am simply the man walking alone in the morning
with a silent figure just behind, neither gaining, nor falling back.

Through The Scrim

Beside the garage-study where I work is a narrow space
bounded by the high fence to my neighbor's property.
It is filled with odds and ends, wood, and metal barrel rings,
an old hand truck, and a tangle of vines
with a multitude of spider webs. All of this is covered
by the scales and tiny seeds from two birch trees
which rain down thickly throughout the Summer.
In the morning fog, this tiny landscape reminds me
of the Victorian bedroom of my great grandmother,
the shades drawn with yellowed lace curtains,
which excluded most of the brilliant Southern California light.

We are, said a friend recently, on the doorstep of old age,
adolescents of this new, final period,
readied to be ushered inside, though our hearts
still beat wildly. I stand, in the mist-heavy morning,
trying to photograph the unruly growth.
I've set up tripod and camera, but am unable to find
the view I want or need. I want light, not dimness,
a flood of sun and water to clean it all away,
a riot of color to destroy all the curtains
and detritus of years, all that's ancient, wise, and dying.

Part 5
Breakfast In Bed

Interminable

After dinner, Naomi said she wanted to sleep with me,
but was too tired that night to make love.
Said we would in the morning,
and kissed me hard, with her tongue,
then quickly fell asleep.
I lay naked and erect next to her soft nakedness
all night in an agony of desire and anticipation.
Once, she murmured, and sighed,
and turned towards me, touching me,
but stayed in deep, dreamless sleep.
Morning finally came, and she woke,
stretched out her arms sleepily
and drew me to her.
Afterwards, she said happily,
it was like having breakfast in bed.

No More Magic Tricks, Only The Real Thing.

One poet I know claims that naming things domesticates them,
that all the wildness and magic in the world is reduced.
Perhaps. But I wonder if Betelgeuse, Loge, the Mariposa Lily,
gneiss, pulled pork, the Castalian Spring and the Mitral Valve
are simply doorways into more mystery, the unknown like a scrim
in front of another in front of a painted backdrop, behind which…

Isolating The Beautiful Things Of The World

Just see how the spider somehow managed
to string his web twenty feet across from the deck railing
to that overhanging branch of the Box Elder,
and then constructed his fine, symmetrical trap
right in the middle, the Summer breeze hardly stirring it,
but the sun making a prism of its strands.
What are the Pyramids to that?

Lives Of The Poets

After the workshop,
he always remembers
to wheel out the garbage
onto the curb. There stands for a moment
in the silent, dark street,
waving goodnight to Steve and Larry,
who are talking by one of their cars
about something
important.

Gnosticism

Sure I cook, because he expects me to,
and the kitchen was remodeled -
but the time it takes! It's the texture
of things - stringy, fibrous, endless chewing
of meat - it's horrible;
my jaw gets exhausted. And lettuce
is such a waste, no nutrients
and it eats slow. Maybe
there's something wrong with me.
Maybe it's just getting older; I don't know.
Chocolate is good, yes, because
it's creamy and goes down quickly.
And toast, though nothing with crusts,
nothing thick. Really, I don't have the time,
I'd prefer to stop eating entirely.

Squirm

To be deeply embarrassed
is merely to reveal
our own vulnerability.
The way animals
never are.

How strange it is
that we can confide
to a friend or stranger
our worst infidelities
but never admit
to stealing a newspaper
from a neighbor's lawn.

Secular Humanism

At the fine restaurant, the chef, appearing after the main course,
explains in detail and with pride how the cattle were slaughtered,
from a distance, individually, with high powered rifles,
so they would not know to be afraid at their deaths,
and the taste of that fear then be found in the flesh.

The Triumph Of Nature

Still nervous about spiders, I whacked the one
that was on the ceiling lamp. Didn't crush it,
but it slowly drifted down, dying but making a web,
half falling, half going somewhere, and then, landing,
crumpled, its legs curled up. The single strand of web remained,
its faint silver reflected in the light.
Defeated by beauty again, I sat down
with the silk thread beside me, and tried to work.

The Terms Of Growing Old

It's a little like trying to explain the game of baseball
to an elderly German in German,
when you can manage the language, but haven't mastered it.

Understanding Fundamentalism

One year, frantic with worry,
my Lady about to leave me
for another man,
I began to destroy my books,
ripping them off the shelves,
throwing them on the floor,
tearing some of them in half.
No books that are not tools,
I shouted to the swirling dust.
I felt like the Taliban
destroying stone Buddhas.
I liked it.

Existential Anxiety

If I pull the covers over me, I get too hot;
if I don't, I will be covered with bites the next morning,
which will get worse for three or four days
and I have no discipline when it comes to scratching.
So I lie awake, waiting for the approaching hum,
flail at it hopelessly in the dark, and then wait again.

One Night In Boston

As she removed her clothes, and got in under the covers,
Becky said to me that happiness is neither the goal of human life,
nor a reasonable expectation.

O.E.D.

It seemed like a good idea, so I signed the form,
and sent the tempting offer back.
The great books duly arrived,
along with the bill, which I threw away.
And kept throwing them away until, one day,
some one stood at my door,
inquiring for a Mr. John Clare.
I'm sorry, I said; *he is, I understand,*
deceased, and the man, clearly frustrated,
but still polite, thanked me, and left.

Foolishness

The reason I never wanted children was a pretty one:
because I wished to be immortal.
I saw how children dragged their parents down,
weighted them with care, forcing them to grow old
in order to take over their space.
Fine for Darwin, I thought,
but not for me.

The Noble Purpose Of Art

I was told once by a music teacher
that the reason we loved Tchaikovsky so much
was that he allowed us not to be ashamed
to feel sorry for ourselves.

Part 6

In The 17th Century

1)

it was understood the brain had hollow chambers,
holes and passages,
            some of them hidden for the dissecting knife
to discover, some clear and open to anyone
       who wished, and had the means,
               to view a split-open head,
        and that in those recesses spirits resided,
        brought there through the air,
inhaled – we were building soul
      as we wandered through the world –
             and grew.
They would stay with us during our lives,
acting like some infusion,
            taking on our color, and our timbre,
becoming, in the vaulted cathedral of the brain's passages
which they had in fact constructed,
      who we were,
      until,
      at our deaths,
they would depart, transformed by their time with us,
and not return.

2)

All the world we know is texture: water and wind,
eroded sandstone, tree, root, earth
and flesh.
How is it possible to tarry so long with the unseen?
Why do we punish ourselves daily over what is unknown?
and unknowable?
      A poet friend says

that if all the pleasure of the world were compressed
        into a numerical scale from 1 to 10,
the first 9 for her would be taken up by eating.
How will the Lord take notice of this tube of flesh?
Unimpeded, the spirits roam through the hollows and coombs
of my mind. They linger in the hanging valleys
constructing strange architectures while I try to live
with what I can touch.

3)

The man who first studied the human brain and realized it was
more than a three pound mass of mush attended the hanging of a
young servant woman who had given birth to an illegitimate child
(the result, almost certainly, of being seduced, or raped, by the son
of the master of the house) and then had either watched it die, or
perhaps killed it. Hangings were public affairs in 1650 in Oxford
and, even though some pleaded to spare her life because of
'extenuating circumstances', the execution proceeded as usual.
These events were a sort of crude and horrific festival. When the
trap was released, the press of people was overwhelming. Some
came up to her and pinched her nipples; others grabbed her
dangling legs and swung on them. There was much laughter and
shouting. Eventually, she was cut down and delivered to the
doctor, who had planned a dissection in front of his students. Just
as he was about to begin, the corpse moaned, and, rattling, began
to breathe.

4)

Perhaps it is foolish
to keeping pounding at the wall

without a code.
                    Speak *Friend*
and enter.
                    An old riddle. Yes,
                    but if you do enter,
are you prepared
                    to accept
                              what lies beyond?
There are some wounds from which you never recover,
friend.

5)

Thomas Willis disconnected parts of the brain in dogs,
stitched the poor beasts up, and observed what happened next.
In this manner, he discovered
how the brain controls different functions.
Most of the dogs died terribly,
though one survived and afterwards
always accompanied him
on his rounds through the city.
The heart is not merely a muscle;
who would dare argue with Tristan?
You cannot dissect what you cannot see.
Dr. Willis was a devout man, who saved the woman,
brought her slowly back to life, and worked to overturn
her conviction, so that she could live,
and later marry, and produce three children.
Who held secret meetings at some risk
during the time of Cromwell, for believers,
including the Archbishop of Canterbury.

6)

So now we think we know the answers, and they are terrible.
There is no real goodness, or what good there is
has no meaning in a random world.
We survive for a while, or we don't.
I suppose the Archbishop would have been wise to suppress him,
but he understood Willis to be a believer,
and paid little attention to what the knife,
and curiosity, revealed. She died in her thirties anyway,
about average, for the time. That is, for someone poor.
The mud wasp builds its chambers, provides food,
lays eggs, and then leaves. The larvae will know what to do,
and you may regard this as an endless monotony
or a miracle, as you choose.

7)

In the Seventeenth Century, they understood the truth,
                    just as we do now.
                    If we transfer
our consciousness,
                    who is it that is transferred?
There are some wounds from which you cannot recover.
Something is always lost.
                    A dog with its head bobbing,
as though it had the palsy, follows me on my rounds.
I do not know the answer.
                    I fear God, but would wish
to love Him.

We walk together in the stinking city,

expecting little, but trying to help.

Human misery is a constant.
                    If we could perfect the brain,
re-wire it to allow us the happiness we deserve,
would that be a good thing?

Part 7
A Truce With Fantasy

After Long Illness

Edward Weston said that a great photographer
should be able to go into his back yard
and find photographs. Not that it's easy,
but the eye must be trained, and the world is limitless.

So I've tried, poking around the garden with my small camera
and tripod. I'm still too weak to go to the mountains,
but if I turn on the sprinklers and take pictures of spider webs
covered in a fine mist, or birch seeds covering old iron,
or the spikes of day lilies thrusting through the rotting fence,
these small victories are the best, the littlest things
most precious. I am trying to rebuild my life.

My time is running out, yet I am, as always,
at the beginning. Studying a blank page
as though it could solve all the mysteries of the world.

From Illness

Wait harder.
—Ernest Hemmingway

Waiting is the only thing I do, the wash of it,
the stillness. I know my life will disappear,
in the wearing away from illness,
the diminishment of waiting and its fruit,
that what I own no longer can be touched,
dissolves as through a scrim when I reach out,
as if preparing something wholly new:
there is no action that is not waiting's triumph.

Yet I lay in the bed, waiting to be myself again,
knowing it might take months or more.
I felt me slip away, and then, as I got better,
forgot – forgot my waiting, though it continues
with every breath. Forgot what to do,
as though my doing were not my affair.
Forgot everything I had learned,
if dissolution is a learning thing.

In those long days, lying on my side, watching
the sun and shadow out my window,
as they changed and darkened through the day,
fearing night and pain, resigned to the tedious days ahead,
the long slow healing, though to what I had no idea,
no feeling, I waited for who knows what.
It seemed enough then, and is all I'll ever know,
being built that way, waiting, forgetting, and waiting.

Recovery

There are words that mean nothing.
But there is something to mean.
—George Oppen

August evenings with the clamor of cicadas
starting up dying down and then even louder
a crescendo and then over again
underneath a whine
                              a higher pitch of crickets
with a full moon rising in the North Carolina night.
Sitting on the porch of our cabin the night swaying
in the heat the thick air the sound
                                        resting after
Goats complain briefly across the valley
other animals stir and settle
                                clouds dissolve into the night
It is not romance we are celebrating here
in the soft air
                    with a glass of cool wine
and the light gleaming on the wet white grass
below us
            We are sleeping then and I wake
in pre-dawn the light ivory
                              get up quietly
                              not to disturb her
hoping there are no nightmares this night
go out the door naked to photograph
the dark shapes of trees and the light
the cicadas endlessly calling
the morning not far off.

Ghosts

I thought it would be fairly easy to find the small, neat house set well back from the road, a white fence, several trees. The front door, under a small porch, we often left open. The cottage behind, which was my study, should also be visible. We had ducks that wandered, during the day, in the front yard, quacking softly, peering into the living room, and then marched back to their cages at dusk, because of the raccoons. Until one day, when they came early, and set up a tremendous noise, and we ran out back too late, and saw one white duck limp in the raccoon's mouth, and the other mottled one ripped apart near the open cage door. We threw rocks and screamed, but it made no difference.

It seemed easy as I walked along, until I noticed that everything had changed. That little trees twenty-five years ago must now be huge, or cut down, and houses remodeled, or torn down and rebuilt. My modest neighborhood near the forest had become expensive. No map could help me as I looked at addresses, hoping at least the numbers might stir something in me, until we gave up and moved away because there was no work, and we needed jobs, and found them in San Francisco. It seemed I could remember almost everything except where, in fact, we lived. I stood in the morning drizzle, wondering.

We lay on the bed reading English mysteries to each other through the long, wet evenings. I worked as a carpenter sometimes. Usually her two boys visited on weekends from San Jose. The boys played, ran shouting through the yards while I hid in the back, trying to write, or read. The damp of Pacific Grove flowed through our bones. For a day or more, they cried when the ducks were killed. I built a couch that converted into two beds. I still have the removable bottom part, for the younger boy, whose body was found in a hot tub after an opening night cast party twenty years later.

128

I stop at a small, shingled house that looks possible. The trees are gone, the yard totally different. But something about it makes me think *maybe*. It is six-thirty in the morning. I can't decide, finally, between it and another, and walk back to the friend's house where I'm staying.

From The Airport

I look back, past the baggage and metal detectors,
and Jane is there, waving to me. I get to the end
and see her still waving. And then I too wave
and finally turn the corner. Feeling the absurd desire
to burst into tears and run back.
The stewardess smiles, says *Guten Tag*.
After I sit down, more or less prepared
for the twelve hour flight, I look out the window,
remembering what Steinbeck's teacher at Stanford said,
and which he never allowed himself to hear:
You are talented, but must beware your sentimentality.
Then, after the meal, fighting off tears at the bad movie
whose name a week later I can no longer remember.
What is this excess of feeling that forces its way out
at the flimsiest excuse? I think of my Father who, if not calm,
rarely showed any emotion other than anger,
evenly describing the cancer they had found in him,
and then getting to the word *malignant*,
and breaking finally down. And, for the rest of his life
often broke down, unable any more to control
the flood of emotion that had waited over sixty years
to reveal itself and, once revealed, would not stop.

Children

I drove all Saturday to Arizona, found the motel in Tucson
she'd told me about, and registered nervously for one,
giving the man four dollars. He looked at me severely
and said *No visitors in the rooms* and I nodded, unable to speak,
half-panicked, the sweat dripping down my sides.
Then, in the room, showered and lay down, looking at the clock.

We were careful, not coming in until after dark,
and not together, she first, with the key. We weren't caught.
But I remember each time the fear. That, and the long trip to
and back from the Reservation the next morning,
a sharp stone of loneliness in my stomach as I contemplated
the fourteen hour drive from Tucson to Sells to Whittier,
driving as the sun finally came up through the tall saguaros,
the light like a strobe while I hurtled down that empty desert road.

A Quiet Thing

As though we'd fallen asleep after hard work,
and awakened in another room,
and recognized this place, dimly, and known it as our own,

and careful, in the narrow gap between two worlds,
we stretched, luxuriating, and slowly became ourselves.

Not desperate, or frantic, no effort to retrieve what never was,
Like breaking open a tangerine, love is piercing, but not loud.

We walked together in the oak hills,
later made love without urgency, as though it was exactly this
and nothing else that was intended.

Love is a quiet thing, so that even the sex in us,
as it climbs to passion and climax, is almost silent,

like snakes entwined which do not move –
nothing wasted, nothing lost –
like the simple things we later do not remember.

Love is like light, its burning so intense that the night yields
to give us color. There is no dark world; there are merely shades.

Over The Moon

In memoriam Stan Rice

The baby's fingernails
                   he said,
                   stopping in the middle of a thought
        were iridescent like an abalone shell
And he held up his fingers
                   as though to show us

I have tried all my life to say something true
        As though these words had the substance of wind
or sunlight blasting the desert pavement
                 I am walking in a small North Carolina town
thinking of the long dead little girl and her father
who was my teacher
He once said that when our civilization is in ruins
they will remember only nursery rhymes
              especially the nonsense ones
Children's books have more terror in them than even Shakespeare
        and they promise more as well
Oh western wynde   the small rain down can rain
My love lies in my arms and I have every reason to be happy

No leaves at all and the light is dark electric at dusk
        and I cannot tell in this soft landscape where west is
until the late glow points it out
They have taken down two houses on Main Street
that were beautiful though falling apart
Others grand even regal with great magnolias out in front
are for sale and cheap
              but would I want to live here

The best way to see an art exhibit he said
is to walk through it without pausing
through one room and then the next and then walk out

133

go home or to a coffee house or something
and see what you remember
I am grateful he liked my Dionysus poem (long discarded)
  It gave me hope
and what a fine painter he became
Childhood is like a forgotten toy that later
  rifling though your mother's things
in one box or another you find
        and pause and put away again

The Lovers Were Doomed No Matter What I Did

Unable to sleep, at 2 am I am fully awake,
trying to change the ending of the movie,
re-living it in a way that would keep the majesty
but jettison the horror.
My mind is a lock; it will not accept.
I will a dream consciously
to make it all come out right,
or at least not disastrous.
Even though love fails,
we should be able to live on.
The wound, though, is all I feel,
and turn from one side to the other,
while my legs ache, and I stiffen,
and realize it will be a long night.

I want to make my life reasonable, but cannot.
I want the one word to be spoken,
the gesture understood in time, and it will not be.
I can't even decide where the turning point is
that could save them.
It seems incredibly important, but it is all a fiction,
and I lie awake for hours
trying to help people who never even existed.
What is wrong with me?

In the gray of early morning, I realize I have slept a little.
The birds begin and there is a quiet.
As a boy, I remember wanting to feel more –
If Tchaikovsky was neurotic, that's what I wanted.
I don't know if the cost is worth it,
nor where it will lead,
but I do know the plot is unchangeable
no matter how much I work and rework it in my dream,
and whatever music we make
will be inadequate to that silence.

Testing Dark

They put me in the boat, secured the ropes, and set it free.
At first it merely drifted in the shallows.
It was the sky I saw, cloudless; also,
an occasional branch reaching out
to remind me of the world I was losing.
And birds, sometimes, flying high above me,
often only heard, their calling no more
than a thread holding me, just barely.
Because I was ready to go, ready to slip out and away
and be carried off, slowly, steadily,
to an end somewhere, an ocean,
where they knew I belonged. And after a time,
it was only rocking, at times gentle, at times fierce.
Then there was nothing I could see any more,
just feel the motion, the sun, the wet.
Not even the birds could hold me now.
Nothing is all I remember, that time, the sweetest time.
Nothing is the core of water, the hole in the sky,
a home without color, the absence of light.

The Return

When I first heard the dogs barking
baying really
                    against the night
I knew the sirens would soon follow
In our world we are encouraged
to do what we do
                    by the sound and smell of animals
We thought we were free of them
We thought we were free of nature
Swallowed the oyster
                    drank the seawater
life-pulse of the creature
devoured pulp and the slimy pit of things
just as our fathers threw sawdust
to congeal the spurting blood
and the patient died anyway or not

But when I followed the clamorous dogs
the sound of the sirens breaking up
like glass shattering
                    splintering like seeds
of a pomegranate along the tiled floor
I thought of Greece and the way
you can hear time moving
across the fields like wind
                    The order of things
turned sideways
                    Athena the Scops Owl

her song a diminished second
called ice-clear across the sweltering valley
and answered and called again
                              each time
a little more dissonant   always
and continually

                measuring backwards.

The Problem Of Language

I wanted to find out what was under the words.
Why we said something
but meant only what we could not understand.
It was just a feint, well-practiced, and even believed in,
though it never helped me get through the night.

I was standing under the redwoods wondering if memory
was better left alone or mined. Everything was silent.
Even the few birds swallowed their songs
and the canopy held steady and the light filtered down
as seen through a scrim. *Speech is the language of desire*,
I said, to no one in particular. But it seemed so foolish,
like a child discovering pleasure, and wanting to repeat it
over and over, before it got old.

Finally, I came back to the little house
and stood before my heart. Beating, pumping,
in spite of what I had done, it had only one question,
and that asked and asked with every beat.
Trees, I thought, trees and the space above the mountain
I would climb, how it always recedes
and the hunger waxes and wanes
and eventually goes out, but still I am asking,
the heart never satisfied, the heart a riot of blood,
and words, and hurt, and sky.

Already After 4

All day sitting in the sun, in the shade.
All day with the cat near me, sometimes complaining,
sometimes sitting on the desk in the little house
where I write, with the door open
and the sounds of my neighbors
sometimes there, sometimes not. All day
waiting to feed the squirrel who now lets me
touch her astonishing gold-flecked fur,
as she eats the seeds and nuts I have offered her,
lets me scratch her head just a little,
while the grumpy cat watches, knowing
there is no chance, no chance at all he can catch her.

All day waiting, wondering at the mystery
and where it begins, waiting and watching the light,
waiting and watching and drifting off,
sleeping as though the real world
were at the edge, not that thing before us,
waiting, without expectation, while the scent
of cooking enters my yard, onions and garlic frying,
sensing how languid death has become,
how sleepy we all are, as the day slows,
falls into a pool of cadmium light,
dissolves out of color and border,
prepares for the long winter night.

The End Of Der Rosenkavalier

If God loves the passionate most,
why does He torment them so?
The happy man has lost his ears.

He looked at his master, probably father,
and lumbered towards the door. The crowd
and creditors raged after them. Alone then,
in the now empty inn, Octavian,
bewildered between the two women,
stood helplessly, not knowing what to do,
a role sung by a mezzo, pretending to be a boy
pretending to be a girl.
It was proven by the clever man
sang the Marschallin sadly,
Listen to your heart while you still can.

After Horace

I guess it's better not to know – be patient
my heart - that other would bring panic.
It doesn't matter anyway, you cannot know.
Our lives are in part open ended, which is a gift.
Those who would offer simple answers
are little more than dream abductors.

This fall day the fog has finally lifted,
the view from my windows almost wild:
tangled branches, hummingbirds at the trumpet vines,
the thump of squirrels on the roof.
I have constructed a paradise for today;
lasting's not the point.

Do not think that wine from the fully ripened grape
is a solace; it is time slowed, time savored.
To learn anything you must drink it down.
That is our partial miracle, our true sustenance.
Make a cookbook with your life.
Your friends are your immortals. Feed them.

A Question Of Degree

In Oz no one dies,
which makes for complications
in the stories, all 32
of which I have just reread.
Baum seems not to have been
quite clear; after all, Dorothy's house
kills the Witch of the East,
as the bucket of water later
melts the Witch of the West.
There are endless contradictions
because, finally,
it is impossible to imagine
immortality, no matter
that we all want it,
and some believe it
and the ego denies it.
A flash of light
between two eternities
some say, but that flash
is always going somewhere,
not like a match which goes out.
In Oz, you can stay as young or old
as you wish, be a baby
forever, or a wise old man
or woman. Which would
you choose? Through which door
would you wish to pass?

A Truce With Fantasy

We all move on the fringes of eternity and are sometimes
granted vistas through the fabric of illusion.
—Ansel Adams

1)

How much I have wanted
there to be a hard nut of self,
a perfect, immutable thing,
the golden pit in the blushed peach —
as in the children's stories,
to bring us safely home,
or be the transforming Prince,
a constant metamorphosis
and yet at the quiet center,
pure, inviolable.

We are not satisfied
with what was given.
More. More, said the poet,
against all reason
and knowledge. But make it real,
real with our longing.
Montaigne said he feared
his idle mind was out of control,
and set to discover how to tame it.
Could I do that? Would
I manage the mystery
of change any better
if I gave up my life
to discipline and order?

2)

The little girl sails in the chicken coop
ripped from its moorings in the storm.
The ship goes on to Australia,
oblivious of whom it has lost,
and when the wind is bored
and wanders off to do mischief
in some other corner of the world,
and the sea quiets, and the moon returns,
she falls asleep until the morning.
What land will meet her?
Who will she become?
It is our dreams that bring us home,
nothing else will do.
No fine, clever argument
that leads to extinction
will stay with us long.
Truth is as flexible
as any child's bones,
though they will snap.

At last, she hears the waves
gently on the deserted sand beach
and sees something green behind:
trees with mysterious fruits,
the distant mountains blue
in the morning haze.
She takes off her shoes
and dries herself in the mild sun.
Perhaps there is a key,
found in the sand
with no gull shrieking overhead.
And that key will lead her

into our own world. She
gets up then and walks to the trees.
She picks a peach,
eats it, and puts the golden pit
in her pocket for another time.

3)

Everything I believe tells me
that none of this is true.
It is a fantasy, good once upon a time
for a lonely child in his room.
But that fantasy became part
of who I am, and its other world
was cut open like a melon,
or with a knife severing the air.
It leaks out from there to here,
a great wind from the empty stars
that will suck us into nothingness.
It will not do, and yet,
these stories are the best I have.
I nurse them, knowing their weakness,
knowing also that without them,
the world is intolerable.

Notes

Poem beginning and ending with lines from James Agee: The poem is
   SURE ON THIS SHINING NIGHT, beautifully set to music
   by Morten Lauridsen.
Back and Forth: There is a partial quote from Tennyson's *ULYSSES,* a
   reference to Tolkien's The Lord of the Rings and to Eliot's Ash
   Wednesday. Also reference to the Medieval desire to cover Europe
   with a thousand churches before the end of the world, presumed to be
   in the year 1000.
After or Before: cf :Yeats' Sailing to Bysantium
The Transition: Gilgamesh, the first poem we know about.
Time and Beauty: see the note for Further Instructions. There is also a
   reference to Mahler's *Das Lied Von der Erde.*
Silence is Imaginary Because the World Never Stops Making Noise:
   The title comes from an article entitled *A Voice from the Past* by Alec
   Wilkinson in the New Yorker of May 19, 2014
Transformations: Amsel is the German name for the European Blackbird,
   a kind of thrush, all black with a yellow beak, similar in shape and
   habit to our American Robin, whose song is almost as beautiful and
   much more common than the Nightingale.
Von Ewiger Liebe: Of Eternal Love, a great Brahms lied, or song. A
   fictional portrait of the young Brahms visiting Robert Schumann after
   his madness, when he was torn between his love and respect for
   Robert and his love for Robert's wife, Clara.
Sigmund in the Desert without Protection: cf. Die Walküre by Wagner
The Achieve: In the second section, the movie is The English Patient. See
   also *The Lovers were Doomed, no Matter what I did.*
The Work: My work has evolved over the years, but for a time, I used to
   organize individual wine sales, pack up the bottles and then deliver
   them or ship them off.
Further Instructions: "That painting" is the Apollo and Marsyas by
   Perugino, which used to be placed right next to the Mona Lisa. The
   painting is small and hard to see because of the press of people
   around the Mona Lisa. It is, however, a painting I've always loved
   and once modeled for. See also Time And Beauty, for another
   reference to that painting.
The Perfect Cat: My free translation of the Rilke quote.

Singing with Annie in the Panament Valley: The Panamint Valley is the dry playa to the west of Death Valley. Very austere, very beautiful. Most of the poems in this section are placed in the Death Valley region. Annie is Annie Lenox, singing in Peter Jackson's *The Return of the King.*

Lives of the Poets: I can't resist mentioning that the workshop referred to was begun in 1966 by Jack Gilbert and Linda Gregg and continues to this day, some of us being original members.

In the 17th Centur:y Based on a true story I heard about first on Public Radio. Part 4, cf. Peter Jackson, The Fellowship of the Ring.

Recovery: You cannot use the term 'white grass' without a nod to George Oppen's beautiful poem *The Forms of Love.*

Over the Moon: Stan was one of my teachers at San Francisco State. I will always be grateful to him, and believe he is one of the finest poets of the generation born in the '40s.

The Lovers were doomed no matter What I Did: cf. The English Patient

Testing Dark: This poem was inspired by Peter Matthiessen's *At Play in the Fields of the Lord.*

After Horace Carpe Diem: of course is the phrase. But in his wonderful book, *Horace and Me,* Harry Eyres translates the phrase quite differently, and I have based my poem on his reading.

A Question of Degree: Based on a recent re-reading of the Oz books, both by Baum and by Ruth Plumly Thompson

A Truce with Fantasy: Much of the poem is based on *Ozma of OZ* (as is the illustration by John R. Neill) by that almost completely misunderstood writer, L. Frank Baum.

About The Author

Bill Mayer was born and raised in Los Angeles. He received his BA and MA from San Francisco State University, studying with Jack Gilbert, Stan Rice, William Dickey and Nanos Valaoritis. In the late '60s, he was invited to join a poetry workshop with Gilbert, Linda Gregg, Larry Felson, George Stanley, Bill Anderson, Wilbur Wood, and others. The workshop persists to this day with some of its original participants.

Mayer has published 5 books of poetry: *Longing*, (Pangaea, 1992), *The Uncertainty Principle* (*Omnidawn*, 2001), *The Deleted Family* (Paroikia, 2004), *Articulate Matter* (Paroikia, 2012) and now *A Truce With Fantasy* (Aldrich Press, Kelsay Books).
Poems have also appeared in a number of magazines: *Caterpiller, Ironwood, The San Francisco Bay Guardian, Montana Gothic, Five Fingers Review, Red Rock Review, Paris Atlantic Poetry Flash, Alimentum,* and *Visions International,* among others. He was included in an anthology of American poets who have lived in Greece, *Kindled Terraces*, edited by Donald Schofield.

Mayer has traveled widely, having spent extended time in Vermont, England, Greece, Hawaii, Monterey, Germany, France, Italy, and Austria. He is also a professional photographer (working with Tony Keppelman on *Hummingbirds*, a photographic essay published by Little-Brown), and an importer of German and Austrian wines. He lives with his wife, Jane McKinne-Mayer, who teaches art history at the California College of the Arts, in Berkeley, California.

Sb/

21572072R00087

Made in the USA
San Bernardino, CA
26 May 2015